To

Karen and Dave
with love from Ruth.

VOICES OF MEMORY

Selected poems of
Oktay Rifat

(One of my favourite
Turkish poets.

R.C.)

Works of Oktay Rifat

With dates of publication and translation of titles

1936	First poems in Varlık magazine	
1941	(With Orhan Veli Kanık & Melih Cevdet Anday)	
	Garip	Peculiar
1945	Güzelleme	Folksong in Praise of a Special Person
1946	Yaşayıp Ölmek: Aşk ve Avarelik Üstüne Şiirler	To Live and Die: Poems on Love and Idleness
1952	Aşağı Yukarı	More or Less
1954	Karga İle Tilki	The Crow and the Fox
1956	Perçemli Sokak	
1958	Aşık Merdiveni	Stairway of Love
1961	Birtakım İnsanlar (Play)	Certain People
1963	Latın Ozanlarından Çeviriler	Translations from Latin Poets
1964	Yunan Antologyası	Greek Anthology
1966	Elleri Var Özgürlüğün	Freedom Has Hands
1966	Kadınlar Arasında (Play)	Among the Women
1969	Şiirler	Poems
1973	Yeni Şiirler	New Poems
1976	Çobanıl Şiirler	Pastoral Poems
1976	Bir Kadının Penceresinden (Novel)	From a Woman's Window
1979	Bir Cıgara İcimi	Having a Smoke
1980	Elifli	Elif Poems
1980	Danaburnu (Novel)	Snapdragon
1982	Denize Doğru Konuşma	Speaking to the Sea
1982	Bay Lear (Novel)	Mr Lear
1984	Dilsiz ve Çıplak	Naked and Dumb
1987	Koca Bir Yaz	A Great Summer
1988	Yağmur Sıkıntısı	Collected Plays

VOICES OF MEMORY

Selected Poems of Oktay Rifat

translated by
Ruth Christie and
Richard McKane

with an introduction by
Talat S. Halman

Rockingham Press

Yapı Kredi Yayınları, Istanbul

Published in 1993
by
The Rockingham Press
11 Musley Lane,
Ware, Herts
SG12 7EN

Copyright in the original poems © Samih Rifat
The English translations:
Copyright © Ruth Christie (R.C.)
Copyright © Richard McKane (R.M.)

British Library Cataloguing-in-Publication Data

A catalogue record for this book
is available from the British Library

ISBN 1 873468 19 9

Printed in Great Britain
by Bemrose Shafron (Printers) Ltd,
Chester

Contents

Acknowledgements

Some of the translations in this book have already been published elsewhere, specifically in the *Turkish Journal of Translation*, 1989, *Anvil New Poets*, 1990, and *Modern Turkish Poetry*, edited by Feyyaz Kayacan Fergar (Rockingham Press) 1992. We gratefully acknowledge the cooperation of the editors concerned and the fine Turkish editions of Oktay Rifat's poems published by Adam.

We would like to thank Oktay Rifat's family for their kind interest and encouragement, and Saliha Paker for her helpful suggestions and comments throughout our work of translating; also Cevat Çapan, a close friend of Oktay, who introduced us both to the poet and the man, and Antonia S. Byatt who read a number of these translations and recognised Oktay Rifat's quality as an important writer.

We thank Talat Halman for his interest in our project and for supplying the authoritative introduction.

We are grateful to James Christie who gave unstintingly of his time and attention to the text and preparation of the manuscript, and to David Perman, our editor, for his enthusiasm for the book and his help in making the selection.

We thank Yapı Kredi Bankası, and Selçuk Altun in particular, for their generosity in making Oktay Rifat's *Voices of Memory* a reality for English readers.

R.C. and R.M.

Introduction

by Talat S. Halman

In the evening breeze in the parish
time is like a birdcage: slowly
and gently it sways in the window
over the back garden of the red-painted house,
the house smelling of tobacco, of bread.
And the birds sing: chipet, chipet, chitalinya.
The sun goes down, we withdraw to our rooms,
the trees, our house, the world, together we gravitate.

This poem, called simply "Poem", translated by his friend, the late Feyyaz Kayacan Fergar, conveys the essence of Oktay Rifat's art. Here is clarity of observation as well as the use of imagination and metaphor, an effortless making of myths by ringing unexpected changes on reality, human nature and language. In his anthology *Modern Turkish Poetry*, Fergar observed that many of "these cameo-like poems encapsulate vast vistas of feeling and thought."

In a poetic career that spanned half a century until his death in 1988, Oktay Rifat stood in the vanguard of modern Turkish poetry — first as an audacious, almost obstreperous rebel, together with his friends Orhan Veli Kanık (1914-1950) and Melih Cevdet Anday (b. 1915), then as an eclectic transformer of styles and language, writing from a self-enforced privacy, and finally a reclusive elder statesman creating a unique synthesis. One could say that these three stages in his writing corresponded roughly to movements going on elsewhere in world literature — to the Socialist-Surrealism of the 1930's and 40's, followed by Obscurantism in which Oktay seemed to evoke echoes of the French poets Apollinaire, Supervielle, Aragon, Éluard, Soupault and Prévert, and ending with what one can only call "Pure Poetry". But one cannot, in all conscience, state that any of these poets were "influences" on Oktay. It is possible that he had read very few

---

Talat S. Halman is Professor and Chairman at the Department of Near Eastern Languages and Literature, New York University. He has published five books of poems in Turkish and two in English, and translated Shakespeare, Faulkner and other writers into Turkish and many Turkish writers into English. He was formerly Turkey's Minister of Culture.

9

of them in depth. As for Eliot and Stevens, he had probably seen only a handful of their poems — in Turkish or French translation.

Oktay Rifat's poetry is, in fact, unique, the result of a very personal development. It defies critical analysis in terms of literary schools or influences. Although in the early phase of his career, he seemed to belong to an emerging school, he stood squarely against any school that confined a poet's aesthetic taste. In 1941 even as he became a member of a triumvirate called the "Garip" (or "Strange") Group and published a collective book, with Kanık and Anday, making its début with a revolutionary Manifesto, he insisted (in the text of the Manifesto itself) that "the idea of literary schools represents an interruption or pause in the flow of time. It is contrary to velocity and action. The only movement that is harmonious with the flow of life and does not thwart the concept of dialectics is the 'no-school movement'."

Originality was Rifat's aspiration from the outset, and he remained firm in his commitment to it until the end of his life. When you read the entire corpus of his work, you know that he owed no debt to any other poet. In five decades of creativity, he went through metamorphoses not on the basis of being susceptible to external influences but on the strength of his own poetic explorations. He probably read very little modern poetry in French or in Turkish translation in the last twenty-five years of his life. He developed, however, a fascination for ancient Greek and Roman poetry, producing two anthologies of his own translations, "Latin Poets" in 1963 and "The Greek Anthology" in 1964. On the other hand, he was never a serious student of Turkish literature of the past, be it classical or folk poetry, and avoided its rigid conventions.

Oktay Rifat was born on 10 June 1914 in Trabzon (Trebizond) where his father was serving as Governor. His father Samih Rifat was not only a top-echelon bureaucrat and later a Member of Parliament, but also a respected poet who turned out fairly polished lyric, philosophical and patriotic poems in a straightforward style free of the artifices and gewgaws many of his contemporaries were enamoured of. One of his major works was a critical translation of *Divan ü Lügat-i Türk* by Mahmud of Kashgar, a "Compendium and Lexicon of Turkish" compiled in 1069.

The family moved to Istanbul when Oktay was five months old. He spent much of his childhood and his early youth in Ankara, where he finished the Ankara Lycée and later obtained a degree in law at Ankara University. In 1937 he went to Paris on a government grant to do his doctorate. He lived in Paris for three years and, when the War broke out, he was forced to return to Turkey without completing his degree. He then worked as a lawyer at the General Directorate of Press and Publications in Ankara, later for the State Railways Administration, until his retirement in 1973.

Few poets in Turkey or elsewhere have led a life as uneventful as Oktay Rifat's. In mid-life he chose the routine of a middle-range bureaucrat and the privacy of his home. Especially after the death in 1950 of his friend Orhan Veli Kanik, he became an isolated figure. He avoided the public eye and had virtually no political involvements. He gave no statements and precious few interviews. He kept a low profile at the office, spending his leisure time at home with his wife and family. Unlike the majority of Turkish writers who seem to revel in highly visible activities and a great deal of socializing, Oktay Rifat preferred the life-style of T. S. Eliot or Wallace Stevens. Past forty, he was seldom seen in public, gave no readings, remained publicity-shy. On very rare occasions did anyone catch a glimpse of him in the company of personal, literary or professional friends. There were dark rumours that he struggled with depression which sometimes had a paralyzing effect on him. Whether this is true or not, he was a retiring gentleman who came alive in his poetic imagination and its challenges.

Perhaps because of his reclusiveness and/or the difficulties involved in interpreting some of his poems, much less critical work has been published about Rifat than any other major poet of his generation. Despite his stature since the late 1940's, despite the great esteem in which he was held in literary circles, critics have chosen not to analyse his work. I fervently hope that the present volume of English translations by Ruth Christie and Richard McKane will have a strong enough impact to inspire some scholars and critics to undertake major studies of Rifat's immensely important work.

By the same token, we know very little about Rifat's personality. His life in the bare outline, of which we have some inklings, seems to have been devoid of dramatic, tragic or joyous events. After the early 1950's he was not even remotely involved in any literary controversy. He was involved in none of the incidents that lend colour to poets' lives — no outrageous behaviour, no scandals, no love affairs, no acts of daring. A quiet life: private, dignified, sequestered. In addition to some fifteen collections of poems, he published three novels (for one of which he won a major award) as well as eight plays, most of which were staged and some also published, and a number of translations. For his poetry, he won three prestigious awards — the Turkish Language Society, Simavi and Necatigil prizes.

Clues to aspects of his personality may be detected in a brief piece he wrote for a 1971 book entitled *Poems Selected by the Poets Themselves*:

"Every occupation other than being a poet seems to me to have secondary significance. I earn my living as a lawyer. I don't like money and assets. To me, it is better to know nothing than to have superficial knowledge. I detest lies and liars, especially those who lie for personal gains. I am a socialist. In my view, poetry, socialism and shying away from lies are the pillars of my personality."

In his *Modern Turkish Poetry*, Fergar recalls their early friendship: "Oktay and I were students in Paris just before the last war. I remember him quoting to me quite often a short poem by Philippe Soupault: *"Monsieur Miroir marchand d'habits / est mort hier soir à Paris. Il fait nuit / il fait noir / il fait nuit-noire à Paris."* It is not the surrealist nature of the poem that Oktay was interested in but its very down-to-earth, almost pedestrian simplicity and the warmth of its sadness. Talking about death and things to wear, Oktay was a good-looking man, always well-dressed, always clean. His constant prayer was: 'Dear God, let there be no holes in my socks if I die unprepared'. But he was not afraid of death. When they asked Hemingway what is death, the reply was "Just another whore". Oktay's approach was different. For him death was "a twin brother and a Universal spoil-sport, all rolled into one." When death came to Oktay Rifat in 1988, he was not unprepared for his "twin brother and universal spoil-sport", had "no holes in his socks". He was waiting stoically.

Yet, fifty years earlier, he had started out with a rebellious spirit. When he joined forces with the *enfants terribles* Orhan Veli Kanık and Melih Cevdet Anday, the three of them were resolved to revamp Turkish poetry. They challenged and berated classical Ottoman poetry with its rigid forms, stale clichés, tired prosodic structure, stringent metaphorical system and detachment from everyday realities. They found the folk poetry of the countryside more authentic and enjoyable, but regarded it as a special fruit beyond the reach and taste of young urban poets. As for their immediate predecessors and tradition-bound contemporaries, most of those had done little more than refine conventional verse. One prominent exception was of course Nazım Hikmet (1902-1961) who, bursting on the scene in the early 1920's had introduced free verse, revolutionized form, substance, and style, and initiated his own romantic and millenarian brand of Marxist-

Leninist aesthetics. Less than twenty years after the emergence of Nazım Hikmet, Kanık, Rifat and Anday launched a new revolution which could be summed up as "poetic realism", but came to be known as "new poetry" or "the first new movement". More specifically, the three young rebels were designated as the "Garip Group", *garip* being an adjective as well as a noun meaning strange or bizarre, a stranger or a person away from home, abandoned, lonely, poor, pitiable, the odd man out, etc. The term was the title of the book they published jointly in 1941 (in which Rifat had twenty short poems, Anday sixteen, and Kanık twenty-four along with two tiny simplistic poems written by Rifat and Kanık together.)

A Manifesto appeared at the beginning of Garip. Its immediate effect was to shock the literary establishment, many members of which savagely attacked it. The Manifesto called for radical, revolutionary changes (with some debt of gratitude to André Breton's "Manifeste du Surréalisme"): About 2,500 words long, it asserted:

"We can arrive at a new appreciation by new ways and means. Squeezing certain theories into familiar old moulds cannot be a new artistic thrust forward. We must alter the whole structure from foundation up. In order to rescue us from the stifling effects of the literatures which have dictated and shaped our tastes and judgments for too many years, we must dump overboard everything that those literatures have taught us. We wish it were possible to dump even language itself, because it threatens our creative efforts by forcing its vocabulary on us when we write poetry."

"Garip" poetry, with Rifat as one of its major figures, stressed the importance of writing *about* and *for* the common man, emphasized the use of free verse and the colloquial idiom, valued concrete image rather than abstract metaphor, made the man in the street its hero, and dealt with social problems in satirical terms. In *Voices of Memory*, the poems selected from *Yaşayip Ölmek, Aşk ve Avarelik Üstüne Şiirler* ("To Live and Die, Poems on Love and Idleness") are from the Garip period. McKane and Christie, however, have chosen, wisely, not to include some of the most simplistic verses in that book.

It is clear in Rifat's early work that, despite all his protestations about "realism in the service of the common man", a spirit of romanticism, albeit in rather subdued form, lingered on. For centuries, Turkish poetry was dominated by romanticism — and I have observed elsewhere that the "Turkish mentality is sentimentality." That spirit dies hard. Notwithstanding the determined efforts of many poets in the latter part of the 20th

Century, it often rears its head in innumerable poems that try desperately to rid themselves of romantic sensibilities. Rifat often succeeded in avoiding sentimentality in his later poetry — especially in what he wrote after the mid-1960's — and he scarcely ever fell prey to maudlin attitudes.

But "Garip" aesthetics seemed no longer satisfying in the 1950's, particularly after Kanık's untimely death in 1950. By the mid-1950's Rifat made a clean break with the movement, going to the opposite extreme of obscurantist, absurd, and sometimes deliberately unintelligible poetry, which appeared to bear a resemblance to the "automatic writing" then fashionable elsewhere in Europe. But his was carefully crafted. The most fascinating, and sometimes frustrating, work in this vein —— "Perçemli Sokak" — does not appear in the present volume. Cypriot-Turkish-British poet Tanar Baybars and I produced an English version of all 51 poems in that cycle in 1971, 15 years after its publication. Baybars added a brief note discussing translation problems and asserting that it "is almost impossible to translate". He also quoted from Rifat's introduction to the book:

"Language is a tool for communication. If we want to tell somebody that a ship is cruising, we bring together the signs of the two concepts as words in the language, ship and cruise. It is the duty of the words in a language to make us visualise reality...To use a language is to communicate through words which evoke in us what we call 'images'... 'The hair of the lamp is wet' has no meaning because a lamp has no hair. The art of using words which is poetry and hence the art of using images, cannot be restricted to images which are possible in reality and therefore meaningful."

Perçemli Sokak proved as revolutionary as the upheaval created by the "Garip" movement in which Rifat was a protagonist. Auden wrote: "Poetry makes nothing happen." In its youthful ambition, the "Garip" Group thought that "Poetry can make everything happen." The Group's hopes for political and social transformation foundered — and the audience (the common people) for whom and in whose language the new realist poetry was written failed to pay attention. Now, Rifat undertook another ambitious strategy — to try to re-make poetry and, in the same move, to re-make everything. The result was neo-cubist. Rifat decomposed language, shapes, concepts, relationships, interactions and reassembled them in new and often startling bizarre configurations. The re-composition may and often does sound irrational, but it tends to make sense in ways that only poetry and music are capable of. Here is a short illustration:

14

The fish flies not knowing its leaf
How can it know the rattle in the mirror
Or the trees at our dinner table
Or the water flowing from the girth swing
Hill and rock and stone

It cannot know for it has no sea nor night
It cannot know the light for it has no land
Clad with the body lichen
Beyond the sheep and the goat
Not showing its eyes the fish flies

To some, this creative strategy, sustained throughout the book-length cycle, seemed like nonsense. There were those who satirised the intractably difficult syntax and relationships. A very astute conservative critic, Professor Mehmet Kaplan, reduced the author's ambitious endeavour to mere "word-play" — "because conceivably he has faith in neither the psychology of the subconscious or Marxism and because he does not enjoy conveying his personal living experiences, he has taken the path of some original games with words." Yet, *Perçemli Sokak* and several other books by Rifat and others were to have a profound effect, almost immediately, on the emergence of a new brave movement which came to be known as "The Second New", a highly complex and dramatically imaginative neo-surrealism. Although Rifat was typically not a member of this group, he was one of its progenitors and remained one of its superheroes and high priests.

Rifat created his impressive synthesis in *Elleri Var Özgürlügün*, ("Freedom Has Hands") which is represented in this volume with many impressive translations. Most of these poems are sensuous and abstract, never effusive in feeling, their political themes always controlled. Many are exquisitely elusive, with a muffled *cri de coeur*. There are skeptical, mordant, even cynical turns of phrase, but one senses little despair. The metaphors are strongly evocative: "the night creeps down the wall like a scorpion."

For a poet who was rumored to have long bouts of depression, Rifat's work is remarkably full of faith in optimism, in the essential goodness of human beings, in the mind's power to hear and to heal. He also exudes unshakeable confidence in the ability of poetry to re-create itself and the world. If one of his eyes has gone to sleep, the other is awake, as he insists.

Although most of his output from the mid-1960's onwards was either spontaneously or consciously universal, Rifat occasionally returned to Ottoman history. In a goodly number of poems, he evokes Byzantium and the Ottoman Empire in masterful terms. Remarkably he utilizes for most of these the sonnet form and some light rhymes. The synthesis becomes more encompassing. There are fascinating returns to roots, not the least of which is that his surprising turns of phrase and paradoxical concepts have their parallels in the imagination of his predecessors. Most Turkish folk-tales start with the formula "A long, long time ago / when the sieve was inside the straw, when the donkey was the town crier / and the camel was the barber..." A famous poem by the Anatolian mystic Yunus Emre (died ca. 1321) has such lines as "I climbed to the branches of a plum tree, / And I helped myself to the grapes up there / I snatched one of the wings of a sparrow / And loaded it on to forty ox-carts / The fish climbed the poplar tree / To gobble the pickles of tar up there." A folk saying goes as follows: "The water buffalo built its nest on a willow branch." Sometimes Rifat echoed this verbal imagination.

Nermin Menemencioğlu, a prominent translator of Turkish poetry into English, observed about Oktay Rifat's background that it is "the Greek anthology rather than the Shah-Name*, his philosophy is European, that of 'socialism with a human face'. His themes are essentially Turkish and his mastery of the language is unsurpassed."

Çobanil Şiirler (Pastoral Poems, 1976), well represented here, provided one more engrossing dimension in Rifat's synthesis, pastoral and idyllic poetry interfused with modern sensibilities. Nature has been ever-present in his aesthetics, not as a pathetic fallacy nor as pantheism, but as a noble joy, the illusions of which transport us into its quintessence. Fauna and flora are both sensuous reality and philosophical affirmation. Rifat says, almost in pride: "I felt the essence of my existence / on sea-urchin rock in the sun." In its survival and regeneration nature triumphs -- and, with it, human nature. When Rifat must ask the question "Am I embracing the laid-out corpse of loneliness?" he knows the answer that nature will give for his redemption.

The collections Rifat published in his last ten years are notable for the eloquence of emotion recollected in tranquillity. There is much resignation

---

* Shah-Name: The great Persian epic poem composed by Firdowsi who
completed it by 1010. For centuries, it served as a model for many
Muslim poets.

to fate, many gentle smiles, and nostalgia for fruits not tasted, for kisses not given.

Ruth Christie and Richard McKane capture all the spectral moods of Oktay Rifat with a compelling force in their English versions. Rifat says in his poem entitled "Inscription", which appears in the present volume: "If you need to write again what you have written / translate it into another language and write..." His English translators have written his poems again — remaining loyal to him, to the individual poems, to the cultural context, to the English language, and to the passions and compassions that ennoble the poetic art.

Oktay Rifat, a towering figure of modern Turkish poetry, who might have won the Nobel Prize if he were writing in some other language, probably sensed that his friendly ghost would haunt the beauty of the world, the powers of poetry to create that world. He said so. But he expressed it in typically unassuming and tender terms:

> *When I'm dead I'll come*
> *I'll leap on a stone and come.*
> *I'll shine in the candle of your room*
> *behind the wet glass.*
> *Through the heart of the shadows*
> *I'll creep*
> *and wait till all's quiet.*
> *I'll not stay for the light of day.*
> *I'll come with the rain.*
> *Wait for me,*
> *I'll be there.*
> *When the hour strikes,*
> *when the Other is gone,*
> *when night descends*
> *I'll come.*

Talat S. Halman
New York City

Key to the translations

The poems in this book are drawn from the six major collections
of poetry which Oktay Rifat published under his own name. This
is indicated at the end of each translation by an abbreviation and
a number, representing the page on which the original is to be
found in the Adam editions — thus the first poem, *Duty*, is
followed by Yaş. 18, indicating that it is on page 18 of Oktay's
Yaşayıp Ölmek—Aşk ve Avarelik Üstüne Şiirler ("To Live and
Die—Poems on Love and Idleness"), published in 1946.

The abbreviations used are:

Yaş.	*Yaşayıp Ölmek—Aşk ve Avarelik Üstüne Şiirler*
	("To Live and Die—Poems on Love and Idleness") 1946
Ell.	Elleri Var Özgürlüğün ("Freedom has Hands") 1966
Çob.	Çobanıl Şiirler ("Pastoral Poems") 1976
Den.	Denize Doğru Konuşma ("Speaking to the Sea") 1982
Dil.	Dilsiz ve Çıplak ("Naked and Dumb") 1984
Koca.	Koca Bir Yaz ("A Great Summer") 1987

Also at the end of each poem are the initials of the translator —
R.C. for Ruth Christie and R.M. for Richard McKane.

DUTY

Blacker than a grape,
waist finer than a needle,
how does the ant climb
the slopes with its burden?

Look at the state of this world,
look at the ruined order,
hatched yesterday,
today the dove of passion.

In the twinkling of an eye
the hawk swoops on the swallows.
When the monster's by the waterside
the gazelle is covered in blood.

I'm carrying the whole burden.
I have to think about each of them one by one,
the young coming into the world
ignorant of the world.

The sun rises in the east — that's for sure —
no surprise.
Then I'm the one who has to worry
when the bee stings a child.

The fox's paw is bloody —
something happens to the lamb.
What is the point, Oktay,
of pain for wolf and bird?

Yaş. 18   R.M.

THE CEMETERY FOR
TURKISH SOLDIERS

I

I'm a sailor in the navy,
fishes ate my eyes.
Seeing and weeping are over for me.
I was tall in my life,
if you don't believe me
look at my clothes.

Someone says — I'm a soldier too,
no different from the other dead.
Once we lived in houses.
Now we're outside the doors,
we pass through the wall.

And another says —
My head still aches
remembering the length of my arms.

Another says —
Don't believe them,
they're all liars,
we don't exist.

II

To enter my room with more ease
they come in the form of dead relations.
I look — it's an uncle or brother.
I look — it's a Polish sergeant
and at once he speaks.

I had a daughter five years old.
She's dead, now we're together.
She's fed-up here,
she can't roll a hoop,
she left her hands behind in Warsaw.

A voice says —
No potatoes to hoe,
no stones to break,
no burdens to carry to market,
I'm at peace here.

One is worried about his wife.
He asks me news from home.

When I died
they took my greatcoat.
I'm cold,
winter's ahead.

Then they speak as one.

III

"We drink water from one glass.
In the evening we eat together,
someone's in love with our loved one,
someone wants to be fostered by our mother."

They come and go at random on the ferries.
They enter our midst on the trams.
It seems they never leave us.   ,
They want to live again a long long time.

Yaş. 19   R.C.

21

CHILD

He died —
he doesn't know he died,
his two hands lie by his side.
They'll carry him away,
nor can he say,
'I won't go!'
He couldn't taste the halva and funeral-cakes.
He couldn't even give thanks
to the friends who bore his coffin.

Ah, his death is like no other's.

Yaş. 25   R.C.

DESTINY

It's torturing me:
I am an accountant
but I can't do Maths.
My favourite food is Prophet's Passion Aubergines —
they don't agree with me.
I know a girl with freckles,
I love her,
she doesn't love me.

Yaş. 33   R.M.

22

LEAVING A CITY

I.   On the last night
      I scattered the violets I bought you
      among the musicians.
      Make my bed once more
      on the morning which starts our last time.

      Little fisherboy,
      you can catch
      playful small-fry from the sea.

      Pretty street-seller,
      I wanted to tell you
      I'm going far away.

II.   Ask the tree
      to bring me its shade —
      a gift for my journey.
      From the window I'd ask for
      the street and the sea.
      From you I'd ask cakes
      shaped like the crescent moon.

III. It's enough that your hands say goodbye.
      Why are you crying?

Yaş. 40   R.C.

ANOTHER TOWN

It's dark up the street
the coffee-house alight,
I like light and idling,
dreaming and rain at night.

It's my delight
to pace the rainy streets,
to stop and stare
and enjoy
the life of street-seller and boy.

I hum a song.
I whistle to the stars
as though the stars and market
belong to me.

The city life for me,
a man of crowds
with companions and friends
and money in my pocket.

To sate
hunger for food and love
I must be free,
then when the fancy moves
I'm off to another town.

Here I grew bored and stale,
so off to another town.
What can this park and pub
mean now to a vagabond soul?

This longing stronger than death
leaves neither sleep nor rest.
Goodbye, my friends, goodbye,
the traveller must move on.

Yaş. 42   R.C.

TWO ROOMS IN A HOTEL

I'm sure like me he makes his morning tea
before he sets off on his daily course.
Who knows what tongue he speaks;
I think he must have come
        from far away.

It is his footsteps I have heard,
sometimes he hums a song.
Oh now, I'll say, he's lying on his bed,
I'll know at that moment
        he is bored.

The nights I fall asleep with thoughts of him
I blanket him in dream,
I wonder if he thinks of me
        as I of him.

A friend who lives in ignorance of me,
I'd be upset if he gave up his room,
a thin-faced, puny youth,
my neighbour — probably a decent man.

Yaş. 45   R.C.

THE WINDOW

My window
a golden lily
opened in the garden of darkness.
A tree tapped on the glass
to pass the night in my room.

Were you shivering there in the cold,
O delicate tree?
Or was it thieves who alarmed you?

Long ago forty thieves bound my hands
in vain.

And the heedless dog at my door
gives no warning,
he's chasing a hare in his dream.
Now in the morning
the clouds oppressing the heart
steal away up the chimney.

Yaş. 48   R.C.

BROTHER

He enters by door and window together.
He brings me gifts.
He's both at the head and the foot of my bed,
and under my bed and in it.

Who is he? Whom does he ask for?
What news does he want to give?
How will he tell his trouble?
Where are his lips? Where are his hands?

He sits in every armchair at once,
aimless he wanders.
He thinks my room is his.
He drinks my water and reads my books.

But in my dreams,
he shows me curious pictures from afar,
trees, mountains, houses, more
and oh — much more!

Yaş. 50   R.C.

THE OLD DAYS

In the old days
the big were still little,
the dead hadn't died yet.
An okka of sugar cost sixty para,
a box of oranges a silver coin;
fruit was abundant,
the larder full.

Nazife — the hamam girl
was pretty and young;
Ali Efendi sold paper and curled his moustache.
In those days too
how they made love!

We got up to such tricks,
but nobody guessed
so smartly we covered our tracks;
Oh the old days!

Yaş. 53   R.C.

SUMMER IN THE CITY

My hands remember a glass,
a glass full of water on the tablecloth.
What I held were my days,
fingers invisible at noon.

Streets of my childhood pass by.
Just now in the coffee-house I'm waiting
my own return from school
with lunchbox and satchel.

The tramcar sings a song
in the square.
The sea's lapping the sides of the ships,
the clouds in the hunters' bags.

And the tinkling bells of the water-sellers,
the siren-shrieks of the city's toy-cars,
in the day the cicadas
or the shady foot of a plane-tree.

Yaş. 54   R.C.

ANGUISH

What do these waters full of stars mean?
The dream I had, this crystal casket,
anguish seeping into me from the waters
and the luminous fish in the coral branches.

Sleep will not let me go from its domain,
the night lit by mother-of-pearl creatures,
the garden under the golden shooting stars,
the well stretching to the mirror of groundless fears.

Gardens, sun and shore are in my daydreams,
the milk-white ships pass over my head,
the atmosphere filtering through the olive branches,
clouds and birds in my so beautiful world.

The dream I had, this crystal casket,
what do these waters full of stars mean?
The luminous fish in the coral branches,
anguish seeping into me from the waters.

Yaş. 58   R.M.

RING

The buds are unopened, dried up on the branch.
Spring brings me anguish.
The seagulls appear in the sky,
but where is the sea I longed for?

Is it me the waves want to drown?
Why do the birds circle in my head?
The shore is a line drawn from sorrow
and the ring is tightening inexorably.

Is my home so very near?
But those in eternal exile,
my dead who come to my window,
line up together with the night.

Is it the garden that harbours the light of the sky?
Where is your home? Tell me —
The ship I left for infinity
is lost in the holy cities it sought.

Now my roads are closed.
Yet my winds are many.
I enjoy my daydream,
That rucksack empty on my back.

Yaş. 59   R.M.

PICTURE

On her green-ivied balcony weary she gazed
at the trees blue and far.
Pensive and quiet,
a book on her knees,
she ran in her daydream
to the golden evenings.

With evening the good days came back.
Seabirds flew to warm shores.
On her colourful shawl were Indian birds
and Japanese charmers on her fan.

Yaş. 64   R.C.

BACK TO HIS BIRTHPLACE

Like trouble that place never leaves my heart,
junipers high and low in its green glens.
I think the swallow in the deep blue sky
wings straight to that country.

Little bird, when you reach that realm
take my endless greetings to the hills,
the goat-bells, udders leaking milk,
the lavender, the bees and beehives.

Where are the white, the snow-white doves,
that peaceful roof amidst the ivy?
The skylark trilled in the high branches
and evening in my window deepened blue.

Ah, with what hopes I used to chase at night
the fireflies' traces;
the trees and sky revolved
in my hoop's mighty wheel.

Like trouble that place never leaves my heart,
junipers high and low in its green glens.
I think the swallow in the deep blue sky
wings straight to that country.

Yaş. 68   R.C.

PLATE

Its whiteness spins and spins
with its lifeless birds
in the midst of nights without end.
The spoon jangles its tune on the plate
at the table
of ancient sorcerers skilled in cruel revels.

Beyond the walnut cupboards
invisible insects devour
the most luminous plates.
When a white dish breaks
Behold! a crimson bud
unfolds in the garden of time.

Yaş.71   R.C.

NOT ME

Am I that little child
schoolbag on back,
pockets bulging with marbles,
dreaming of cops and robbers?

Is that really me? Sweating and gulping water,
falling ill.
Where's the fever I had?
Where's the one who cried by my bed?

If this sailor's shirt is mine
then why are the sleeves too short?
This is your glove, you say.
Look, it won't fit my hand.

Where's my kite with its frilly tail,
my wooden sword and my trumpet?
These pictures are not like me,
I must be a different man.

I'm another person — quite different —
that child is another child.
And the writer of these lines
lived only for a moment.

Yaş. 84   R.C.

TO MY WIFE

You bring coolness to the halls,
a sense of space to rooms.
To wake in your bed in the morning
gives me daylong joy.

We are two halves of the apple.
Our day and night,
our house and home are one.
Happiness is a meadow.
Where you tread
it springs to life.
Loneliness comes from the road you go down.

Yaş. 93   R.C.

36

LAMENT

First your outer covering wore away,
your flesh, your eyes and eyebrows wore away.
Whatever you knew as fresh and young, burned out,
                                    burned out.

Hand and foot you lost, my friend,
pen-slim finger and nail.
Life and spirit once were yours,
                        now lost and gone,
what's left of you, my friend, reduced
                                to lines in books.
— Where lashes, hair and skin?

O shoddy world!
— But once an Orhan Veli lived.
Come, brother Orhan, come,
                        take my hands,
                        use my eyes.

Yaş. 129   R.C.

37

LAST WORD

Value that water
gurgling down your throat.
This blueness beyond words
reaches from the window far as you can see.
Value the sky,
value the flowering almond,
the sunny room and muddy street.
White, black, green, rose,
value them too.
Life beats in the heart with joy.
The poplar winds blow in our heads.
Man is angry, he rages and fights
in a battle fought for the people.
Value that fearful joy
and rage.
Know this
and know its truth:
the sun warms only the living.
Value the sun.

Yaş. 130   R.C.

I SAW MY HAND

Drinking water, I saw my hand,
pink, hollowed and lightly downed.
I said — hello there, hand, hello!
Hold glass and fork and pen
and when the time comes
don't hesitate
to hold the sword and gun.
Stand firm, my hero, my lion-hearted friend.

Drinking water, I saw my hand,
speechless and dry
like Ahmet's hand or Mehmet's.
Hello, I said, hello you busy hands,
that make trains run, I said,
and electricity work.
You topple mountains,
bring water to the dams,
equip the earth from end to end,
make green the land,
empower the human race.

Drinking water, I saw my hand,
no eyes and ears, alive,
his fine blue veins,
the thumb with pleasure bent,
forefinger nicely crooked,
ring-finger inexplicable,
and the little one in a world of its own.

Yaş. 148   R.C.

IN THE ROWING BOAT

Look at this weather, Captain, look at that water.
The sea is like a woman, come off it!
It's better than Marika this bloody sea,
one could commit murder on such a day,
on our left the nets, and on our right the islands.
I was rowing and Mehmet was opposite,
the blue had gone to my head.

Mehmet, I said, heh Mehmet,
light and throw the dynamite.
The black-eye, the bream, the mackerel float to the surface.

I'll never forget that day
on the island on Christ's Mountain,
the sea like a plate before us,
Mother of Pearl Island, Maden and the rest:
I've never seen anything like it all my life.
There was a rustling in the air so fearful,
thousand upon thousand of storks
returning above us to Istanbul.

I understood it again on the sea,
stretched out in the rowing boat I closed my eyes.
To be alive is so good,
it's worth fighting for this life and one can die by good luck
                                                    or fate.
I understood that love of freedom and love of peace
are the same as the joy of living.
Our days are fresh with this belief
and for this the sky is blue and sparkling, sparkling.

Yaş. 149   R.M.

THE EMBRACE

Warm me this night,
O my trust in freedom
wrap me warm
against my mattress thin and blanket torn.
Out there is unimaginable cold and wind,
outside — oppression,
torture,
out there — death.
O my trust in freedom
enter deep,
warm me through this night.
On my palm a place is ready
for your hands,
on my thighs a place
to lean your knees.
Enclose me,
sheathe me,
wrap me warm,
O my trust in freedom
wrap me warm this night.

Yaş. 154   R.C.

41

A NAKED MAN

A man,
a naked man,
a stark-naked man
was about to jump into the sea.
Where from?
From Moda,
from a rowboat at Moda,
the sky an amazing blue,
the sea
like silk.
A man,
one with a big moustache,
astride a quayside bollard,
shouts from the other shore.

> I'm Hadji — son of Tanash the Grocer,
> barkeeper at the Fishmarket.
> Hey, I tell you,
> take care,
> don't jump!
> Perhaps you can't swim.
> I'm only trying to help.
> Don't jump, my friend, don't jump.
> You'll grieve your poor mother,
> and think of your youth.

A man,
a naked man,
a stark-naked man
was about to jump into the sea
from Moda.
A woman shouts from the other shore.

Don't jump, my son, don't jump!
What good will it do?
Slip into the water like everyone else,
you can't afford to jump.
Who'll take care of your family?
and pay Tanash the Grocer's bill?
Don't jump, my child!
We'll be in disgrace with the grocer and all.

A man,
a naked man,
a stark-naked man
was about to jump into the sea
from Moda,
the sky an amazing blue,
the sea
Like silk.
A frantic woman and Hadji the Grocer's son
yell from the other shore.

Don't jump, you treacherous fool,
You obstinate, selfish wretch!
We'll get a bad name.
Don't jump!
It's not fair to us
or to your dependents,
or Tanash the Grocer.

Yaş. 158   R.C.

PINK HOUSE ON THE BOSPHORUS

There are girls crisp as lettuce,
their mouths and noses curved and curled.
They sit cross-legged on the ferries,
the wind blows, and when he looks
a man has glimpses which make his heart pound.

Oh Istanbul, old devil that you are!
Down at Findikli there's fun and games.
A line in my hand with a hundred hooks,
I plunge like the North wind among the tunny
from Captain Turgut's boat.

I've never been to visit Orhan's grave
at Rumelihisar,
I never want to go.
Now with fresh bread, a morsel of white cheese,
he'd be just here,
drinking raki and watching the sea.

I leap from the quay to the water,
fish below me,
clouds above.
The choppy Bosphorus laps by my mouth.
I swim straight to the pink house on the water's edge.

Yaş. 155   R.C. & R.M.

A TIME UPON A TIME

You came up on me from behind every tree.
There were so many of you that I got depressed from loneliness.
Your mad wind blew the mountains and rocks
and flung the staircase I leaned on against the towers.

You came out at me at every corner,
but you were so absent I cried and went mad.
The stones were thinned with your blood,
the clouds recalled the old seas.

What a shame all your countless yous had gone.
It was as though you had been in a time upon a time.
I stretched out and from where I was softly caught the sky
that you had thrown.

Yaş. 230   R.M.

YOU

When I come down the Street of Steep Steps
you are my stairs.
Among the crowds I walk you.
You are they.
I think but thinking's empty.
Looking is best: at you,
the blue of the tunny,
you the boat,
the seabird,
pillars of the Bridge,
the unhappy poor
are you and all are you.
A woman brushes by.
Beyond you there is only you
who pass
who go.

Yaş. 232   R.C.

SUMMER WINDOW

The barefoot orphans inside
are sharing hot bread on their knees,
seeing in their blindness,
knowing in their ignorance
love triangles in the air.

Yaş. 239   R.M.

46

FREEDOM HAS HANDS

1

Our horses galloped foaming
to the calm sea.

2

What is this flight? Is it the dove's
joy of freedom?

3

It was forbidden to kiss, did you know,
forbidden to think,
forbidden to defend the work force.

4

They've picked the fruit from the tree
and they sell it in the market
for as much as they can get,
labour's broken branches on the ground.

5

Light is blinding, they say,
and freedom is explosive.
Arsonists smash our lamps
and with oily rags set fire to freedom.

As soon as we reach out, they want an explosion,
and they want us to catch fire when we light the flame.
There are mine-fields,
bread and water wait in the darkness.

6

Freedom has hands,
eyes, feet;
to wipe the bloody sweat,
to look at tomorrows,
heading straight for equality.

7

I'm the cage, you are the ivy;
tangle, tangle as much as you are able!

8

Love of freedom is this:
once you're tempted there's no escape,
it's a habit that never gets old,
a dream that is truer than reality.

9

The historic flow of brave herdsmen,
the workers, bees of the universe's beehive;
milling round black bread,
brothers who bring freedom to our world.
By that bread the mind is roused from sleep,
our endless night dawns with that bread;
people attain independence with that sun.

10

This hope is the door to freedom,
half-open to happy days.
This joy is the light of happy days,   *
gently, timidly its rays strike us.

Come people of my land, show yourselves
like a budding branch at the door of freedom,
and behind you the sky is brotherly blue.

Ell. 9   R.M.

A BIRD

The time when clocks are most precise.
Evening: a bird motionless in the air.
The town freshens its make-up in the mirrors.
The street is as our heart would want it, faultless, perfect.
We are silent, completely alone, tea, a cigarette and a pen.

Ell. 49   R.M.

CAT NIGHT

I went out in the garden at midnight:
the cat came out after me.
The sea was like a mill-pond, indescribable,
the stars like the cat's eyes.
A black-mulberry tree was just over there,
shadowless, quivering, just over there;
the cat looked at me from above.
I thought of you all, bitter, sour.
The birds sang, the ferry whistled.
        Or did I imagine it?

Ell. 93   R.M.

REVOLVING

It's you revolving on my axis, not the world.
One of my faces is your day, one of my faces your night.

Ell. 102   R.M.

STREET

In a street narrowed as a cat's eye,
the slippery rope of rain on my shoulder,
I drag an old corpse on the spare horse.

I revolve round the axis of my phantom,
like opening a door for myself.
One of my eyes has gone to sleep, the other is awake.

The night creeps down the wall like a scorpion.

Ell. 107   R.M.

THE BIRD

In an antique mirror my self was becoming many: one of me
spawned ten, ten twenty: my crowd of selves enlarged.
Baker, blacksmith, soapseller, publican;
I was sea, street, the tree and loneliness.
From the glass I was drinking myself, taking bites
of myself in the apple. Lie down, get up, sleep, wake,
I inside the selves I scattered about me.
Later the sun sank, purple darkened behind the hills,
a bird sang on the plain, from a different stuff of creation,
echoing like moonlight reflected in our mirror.

Ell. 108   R.C.

50

WAITING FOR ME

They wait for me,
the sea, the streets, my love;
I carve my name on a tree
which swims like a deer in the summer lake.
My star was a bell that rang, and then went silent.
My shoe was worn to holes on the pebble of dreams.
I lay on my back in the rough fields.
Goat-bearded demons, throng about my head!
The creature in the box lies in wait,
the one whose back is turned
          waits for me.

Every leaf is an ant, the sky flocks to the plain.
When the harvest of blood-red rye has begun
and the cloud a sparrowhawk, perches
on the windlass of the well
where the terebinth-berries grow,
the broody hen swells.
Time and the wave ebb and flow.
The warm smell of the sun baking in the evening ovens
strikes on the weary stones.
At the doorways the women mend with their long needles
the cloth left half-devoured by the bat.

Work quickly, women, quick,
the blue mare's flanks await me.

Ell. 120   R.C.

THE RAINS

Then the rains began, the acrobats left.
The traces of tents were erased from the plain.
Orange-painted boy, blue-breasted girl,
what became of them? How fast they vanished!
A smile from summer lingered on the walls,
and with dead photographs they blew about the street.
They flew rather than walked, their hands
wide open with the sun.
They urged us, pensive and sad,
to lightness.
Prudent and skilled were they, we absent-minded,
careless, trailing their dreams.
From now, whatever is,
is empty, dirty, rotting-soft.
The sky with its regal mountains of cloud,
purple and round, rough as the sea,
dragging the migrant birds by the hair,
is moving like a hostile army overhead.
        The rains have begun.

Ell. 122   R.C.

TABLE

I set the table on the slope of night.
      On my left the moon rose, on my right
the sun set. The peacock of the sky opened
      its tail on the perch of a star
and a rose-coloured light struck my bottle.
      Sip after sip I got drunk:
unlived Time in a locked chest
      wore out like unworn clothes.
The future of my days is clear, their past — empty,
      numbered by the flickerings of the candle.

Ell. 131   R.M.

FACES

It was as though they were really they,
I was really I, as though I really existed,
they embraced me, kissed me when they came and went.
I forgot their faces, I placed a star
in the gaps, as though not all my stars
were dead, as though the faces were real.

Ell. 141   R.M.

NIGHT AND DAY

Nights under the light of the lamp,
days by the poles of the fish traps,
eyes blue from looking at the sea.

Ell. 144   R.M.

OLD POEMS

I looked at the lofty trees, I wandered about,
I thought: Oh where can it be?
On earth or in heaven? Stones and bees,
grass and sunlight, mystery of mysteries,
stayed silent with their secret fragrance.
I sang the old poems from the beginning
to the village of the ancient dead.

Ell. 145   R.C.

TWO MEN

Where have you come from? Your face and eyes
puffed as a loaf, your clothes soaking wet.
Outside like a wounded jackal
the forest howling and raging,
and moving clouds hammering nails of rain into the earth.
Come and sit in the light of my lamp:
pull up the heater, get warm!
Here's soup, crumble bread in it.
Speak, though you falter, break silence.
Scatter love's wheat in my field!
Let the plain open the flowers of spring!
Adrift in the middle of darkness a light
and face to face — two men.

Ell. 146   R.C.

54

FACE TO FACE

Face to face with a tree I stood and looked
from a window opening on darkness,
an indescribable river was flowing past.
In the water
a thousand-shafted star was swimming and flashing,
and a mountain, high,
held a path leading to distant places.
>   You could hear sounds,
>   unknown sounds.
>   Nothing appeared beyond.

Ell. 151   R.C.

55

WINDSWEPT

I pitched a tent on windswept images.
Fitfully I live in my skies.
I come down to the sea by mountain paths.
I'm in the loneliness of stone, but living,
I'm in the whiteness of milk, but clear.
Beyond the fence a star rises and grows.
My sheep seem to stray but return.
On the pointed crag
the goat stands still as stone
against the blue-veined light.
I gather the sound of bells in my pouch.
I strike a match,
the red flame of the yellowed grass
warms my heart.
I've no-one to bring me a bowl of soup,
no girl, no mare!
no friend but that pipe.
I play my pipe for the clouds.
The mountains and plains draw near.
See, mountains!
this tune is for you, and this one for the plains.

Ell. 164   R.C.

56

YOU IN YOUR LONELINESS

I

You — in your loneliness and fear,
locked into fables, outside time;
in the timid half-world of copper jugs,
buckets and torn kilims;
an old crooked tree that gives no fruit,
propped up against hollyoak hedges.
But I am one of the unhappy, out-of-work, broken men
from the black-visaged towns,
before your shacks and tents,
and the oil lamp smoking in your night,
looking at each other in silence,
not reaching out, not joining,
dissolving, melting in the darkness.

II

My green-crested duck, come land
on my lakes, the hunters are off to the mountains!
Here's the sun like a lusty bull
grazing in the meadow of the sky,
the hot sand, here's the fish slipping through the reeds.
Here's summer, clouds and clover,
the spacious plains, the plains all over.

III

Yours is the pain, the love and the hope.
The sap that opens the bud to the sun
rises from you, rises to my branch.
When you till my earth with your simple plough,
the most sacred of greens, the wheat,
grows a tender sprout.
The seeds of tomorrow foam in your sea
and spread to the waste lands
with harmony, order and light.

IV

I bound myself with you to tree
and stone. Without you I am a cut rope,
a dry well, alien to nature, to love,
an alien in the most beautiful plain,
displaced, meaningless, unnecessary, distant.
Embrace me in my unhappiness, hold me!
The day unborn, the sky is empty,
tremulous as an oil lamp, the smoky Night
comes gently in from the west.

V

So even if your rivers rage and foam,
there's still a willow's shadow on the bank,
enough for me. You have a tongue, a mouth.
But I have my goats, glassy-eyed, that I herd on the mountains,
mallow and edible plants in my meadows.
I tenderly hold a cooing dove to my breast.
Come, let's light a fire, open our bundles
and share tobacco and bread side by side!
Bring down your eagle face from high mountains to plain,
and let our sun filter through the willow branches.

VI

If only it would wake, we thought, and be all eyes —
a vast poppy field, just eyes
alive with sympathy and sacred promise.
The night has passed in waiting. There is no dawn.
If only the streaming rain would pour from the sky,
weaving nets to catch lice and scorpions.
We who patiently grind the wheat,
we who slice great chunks of bread,
our cheeks are sunken, our faces pale.
Like curled-up woodlice, we reproduce under a stone without loving,
and we can never get rid of the couch grass in our fields.

If only the seed sown with light
would multiply with lightning, we thought.
But it's always we who must give!
We loved the forest that soothed our days,
but what a tongue of flame is this naked plain!
Let the poplar fall headlong,
and our prison birds fly away and settle elsewhere!
The soul is empty, hope stunted and blind, the depth
of the wells cannot be gauged. Let the sun be ours,
this earth, this branch, this fruit!

VII

Looking down on the plain from the windy peak,
you are a bird flying beneath me, an oak forest on your flank.
You are a mountain with ploughed foothills.
You are blue, a cloud and space, from one summit
to another. You are a little windmill,
you are a stream foaming in a mossy gully,
the teat that lambs suck, the tremble of a leaf,
a breeze in a willow branch.
I gave birth to your taste and colour,
before I knew you.
You are the snow, flake on flake,
weighing down the pines at Rocky Pass.
You are a hut smelling of cotton seed and summer,
bound together with laurel branches,
you are the sun, white milk
from the sweet basil on the heights,
you are an avalanche about to fall,
the pouring rain and the flood, the dark song of the river.
You are the fruit I bite, the clover, the arm
that hugs and the tongue and language that makes me think.
You are thunderous, wild, fickle,
as I gaze at you from the windy peak.

Ell. 175   R.M. & R.C.

THEN TURN

Give what you have in your hand, then turn to the one you've given joy,
look at the face of happiness! It's your own face reflected
        smiling and radiant, in the mirror.

El. 184   R.M.

ALMONDS

The chirruping and smell of the South wind
seduces the childish almonds each year,
circling the branches with its steam they blossom too early.
The bud leaps from sleep, the almonds
are decked out like brides in midwinter.
That fresh fire is like first love,
it's a drop of sun, behind the mountain,
all at once it fell on the plain, it burned,
it was a tree or a man or whoever — it was deceived into blossom.

Ell. 185   R.M.

A SUN WHICH FIRES A PASSION

There are loves that finish as soon as they start;
there are sour tastes that linger in the mouth;
but a sun which fires a passion does not easily sink.
The thousand-branched candlestick burns,
the windows of the heavenly mansion flame on your horizon
and in the purplish haze of honeysuckle
that smokes like a summer evening's incense,
on the balcony over your garden there wait
sweet-smelling crimson roses and vines,
Japanese lanterns, sadness in their midst.
There are days like that, and moments, never-ending!
What light they absorbed from your love!
Suddenly with a new beauty, they broke off
from the Great River, and dropped one by one from the garland.
The showers of spring and longing
opened wild flowers in your field.
Those immortal days, nourished on a nothing;
doves outside time, unable to fly;
plains beyond space, untrodden;
another branch, another season, other fruit.
Whoever treads that earth and tastes that fruit
will be drunk with ecstasy, the jar will fill with honey,
the lock will open that cannot open,
the almond-tree will stay in flower,
wisdom and happiness will twine about the heart.
A white cloud hovers above you,
birds swoop; suddenly motion stops,
not a sound from creation,
you are at the centre,
the pool, the tree, the sea are all for you.
Look, light for you!
When you turn off the sun, you set fire to the sky.
So, later, that day
when you were in quiet deep meditation,
confronting mysteries in a little arbour,
will remain in your mind,
like a picture taken long ago,
shadowless, clear.

Ell. 186   R.C.

POMEGRANATE

Prolific once as a pomegranate full of seeds,
what became of you!
You set off for the mountain with forty steeds
and came back with a hundred.
Your bullet-shots were endless,
your horse reared, your whiplash whistled.
You were pirate or captain or cabin-boy when you wished,
at your side were seabird and cloud, the high seas.
In the harbour you leant on the wine-casks,
and watched the barges of Time
slide quietly, stringing from east to west.
You were a hunter catching a hare by the ear,
you drew out days from between the stones of the past.
From the top of Byzantium's walls
an Ottoman past fell into your hands.
Your face caressed worn beams.
Where now are the rusty grappling-hooks and nails!
What became of the house where the cats made love on the roof,
the backstreet where the wind scattered its salty feathers!
The children in your dreams
like dead caiques drawn up on the beach,
lost long ago in their nightless eyes
that rage like a blue and green sun.
The slim-stemmed glasses are broken.
Behind the dusty panes the fuchsia-flowers burned up.
Outskirts of Istanbul! Days of spring,
misty and warm, old bay-windows;
a girl's face, a horse's crest,
and the axle of a horse-drawn carriage,
glimpsed from a coffee-house bench.

The wall continues the length of silence.
Here and there you gathered a tapestry rose for your bag,
an oleander branch, and joys and loves.
When the poems swarmed into your head
on the sea-smelling roads,
you were like that happy tree,
a flight of sparrows descending about you.
What became of you!
Now you've run out; you've turned to a waterless mill!

Ell. 188   R.C.

ONE THOUSAND LEAVES

The trees grew taller tonight. One thousand
tiny tiny leaves began to grow and imperceptibly
the corn lengthened. The planet earth
entered Aries. A cloud descended
and tonight the earth was wet with early summer rain.

Ell. 191   R.M.

BIRDS OF THE SUN

They are birds of the sun, they settle on the water
and wet weeds. They sing of the skin
of fish, scale on scale fluttering in the nets.
They rock on the playful cradle of drops
and fall like autumn leaves
on the evening-spread plain of the sea.
Shadows withdraw, memories approach,
and hold out dry, dead roses.
Who for? Empty dreams
like the back of mirrors, corroded by the night,
carved and riddled by salt and wind.

The dawn descends on the wet cold rocks,
the wheel of the merry-go-round starts to revolve,
blue bead-eyed wooden horses come and go,
galloping with the iron bit between their teeth.
The long tails and manes, strand on strand whining
fly on the air in vicious circles.
Here is loneliness of roofs, here is longing,
here is sadness, runnings to and fro, waitings!
They pass, the sickle of twin beacons
reaping the puny rye of our flesh.
The swallow flies, dreams do not wait for evening.
Hey, unblown whistling reed-pipe, behind what mountain
are the sheep? From what upland pasture is this scent
of rubbed thyme in my jug of milk?
From what teat is this foam? Oblivious blind men
stretching their sticks to the face of the sky
show the unshown. It doesn't exist!
The blue bead-eyed, dawn-maned horses fall,
strand on strand whining, and from those tails and manes
not even an echo remains in the windy plain.
Grasshoppers of rain jump on the water.
Passions fall, loneliness, deepness fall.

Ell. 192   R.M.

A CRAFTY GIPSY

He made hundreds of whistles from the willow branch,
a crafty gipsy in a horse cart.
We went down to the gipsy camp in the meadow,
with stolen scrap-metal and daisies.
A sunny wind was blowing, the weather was warm.

On roads humping down, overlooking the sea,
on both sides of us flowers of mallow and patience;
lie out on the wet grass if you want, walk about if you want.
The sheepdog is stealthily following us,
he stops, pisses, sniffs under the pebbles.

My tree rustles at the slightest breeze,
a crow drops like lightning
from the top of the pine.
My heart leaps.
The sky, three or four clouds, evening strangeness,
what else is left us in this lying world?

Ell. 194   R.M.

OPEN YOUR HANDS

Open your hands! Open all the closed doors!
Before you catch sky or light it passes,
bring on the sun's flood of corpses.
This river flows from nature. This spurting,
this shaking comes from the plain, more transparent
than the sound of water. Hundreds of olives.
Buried in steam the other side of the field
wild weeds begin at the ditch. Then the fence
and old chestnut trees with thick bark.
This wind comes from the aged chestnuts.
Look at the swollen earth! Plants like fingers,
with leaves the size of pinheads
in their green joy. Turn your face
to the expanse, see yourself in that mirror!

Ell. 195   R.M.

LIKE LOOKING IN A MIRROR

Like looking in a mirror, I look at them,
I tell their stories and find myself.
Let me say, the Judas tree on its sky bed
just before dawn combs its hair
with a coral comb before the cloud's first blush.
Let me say, the vixen with her hesitant tongue
licks its cub swaddled in night,
closing its timid brown eyes.
These images are a still pool with leaf and grass
where I look at my face, perhaps a key
        forcing a rusty lock.

Ell. 196   R.M.

THEY CAME DOWN ONE AFTER ANOTHER

They came down one after another from the forest in our midst,
they grew all over the mountains, all over the stream banks,
spears of light radiating from the sky.
The poplar was straight, thin and tall, the plane — spreading.
They reflected in water, above the reeds, the rushes,
some weeping willows, some pines, some maples.
The trains go by, the carts run on.
Let us remember their names with the life-giving rain,
this blue, this sun, this earth for ever and ever!

Ell. 197   R.M.

IN THE GARDEN

We closed ourselves off from the night with a candle.
We pitched this tent in our garden by candlelight
deep red. We forgot the sky full of fear as a garden-well.
Behind us the forest, its trees
thick-barked and gnarled, oozing resinous streams.
From there comes this smell of leaf and grass.
That's an owl you heard, not a fairy-tale bird.
Only the moths draw close,
not marten, field-mouse or insect.
Come quietly down from the stairway of fear,
turn your face hidden in darkness to me.
Speak! Cut the wild weeds of silence
that grow knee-high at a breath.
The night is damp and fine, but your face lit-up,
your face is more beautiful than light or night!

Ell. 198   R.C.

SUDDENLY

The clocks that stopped long ago
like bats hanging in distant summers,
suddenly started chiming past time.
The needling ants and voices of memory
crawl on my flesh. Night falls on me,
spade on spade of sticky earth.
An iron wheel revolves on stone,
the cart drawn by regrets approaches my door.
Why is the coffin being lowered with its top open?
Where has this nail come from? Or am I embracing
the laid-out corpse of loneliness?
Longing, tail between its legs, lifts its nose
and howls. I stroke its coat gently.
A brick slips from the tower, the mirror cracks.
A pus-coloured moon rolls over the roofs.
In the wet windows lit by lightning
distorted faces appear: you, all you!

Ell. 199   R.M.

A ROUGH PILLOW

Where were we? How were we? — now it's impossible to tell.
It was a rough pillow we shared!
It was us or perhaps someone else who was like us,
the fruit of our love, the immortal child.

Soaking wet from the rain of those dreams,
our coming smeared with sticky blood
will never go out of my mind,
the gentle pulling out like swimming
in the clear sunny waters of the days,
turning into ourselves from our mother's womb,
that first scream, that first blue, that first breath of air.

Ell. 200   R.M.

68

OAK IN THE WIND

Those were splendid days!
You warmed me like the sun.
Time whitened with the happiness you brought,
turned red with the poppy.
Along the way the sour blackberries
sweetened to honey.
A woman herded her geese, cackling and flapping their wings,
a moaning wind drove smoky clouds across the sky.
Waist-deep in grass, a Thumbelina girl
gathered flowers.
We set out for the mountain on the winding path,
we came down from the mountain, shoulder to shoulder with the oaks,
we passed the gate entwined with the forest.
Day met with night, the pitcher cooled at the window.
The white cloth on the table, the copper bucket;
later your face by lamplight, pale and fine.
Shadows on the wall, impassable hedgerows,
the ivy of your hands and lashes,
your hair blowing in the night.

Ell. 203   R.C.

THOSE PLACES

They were poor districts mostly,
but what lively names they had!
Their syllables recalled the familiar chime of a clock,
you shivered when it struck.
What summers those were!
The garden full of poppies, daisies, cornflowers,
the people were different people, their faces different!
Young widows in headscarves and raw silk cloaks,
slim girls and youths.
Who were they? What became of them? Are they dead?
The beautiful Queen of Diamonds, her fortune
told by the cards
came up with the King of Spades; that meant separation.
And now it will finish in tears,
weeping and laughing, sighs,
falling in fainting-fits in the halls.
In summer the shutters were opened wide,
in winter rugs covered the doors.
And a young man shot himself for a girl.
The girl took to her bed and waned.
Those passionate letters, those secret meetings among the laurels,
love-making and promises in the moonlight!
'Strike me blind if I smell a rose sweeter than you!
'I swear on my life,
I'll never love anyone more than you.'
They were in heaven but we on the earth.

We had our garden and balcony: but nothing to theirs;
our entrance-hall smelt of tobacco-tar and cigarette-smoke,
theirs of sage-tea and aloes.
I always caught that perfume in the evening wind
even purer as it rose.
That headiness never left me;
then and now the fragrance turns me dizzy.

Clearly they're still the same,
dim-lit house, hidden path,
the fisherman still an old rascal,
honeysuckle hanging from the stone wall,
and girls in clogs chewing gum at sunset;
roofs and clouds in the water,
and flights of seagulls swarming on the hillside.
We are the ones who change.
There childhood stays, with us it slowly dies;
like trees shedding their leaves,
dreams beyond the small moments of happiness
are stripped of their green, their blue.
Only the branches remain, dry twigs.

Ell. 212   R.C.

FISH AND BREAD

Fish and bread! Sea and cloud, water and sun
and a child barefoot, a brazier hanging
from an iron bar, belching smoke.
He looks at the fullness of the garden; the house
is hidden behind a hot smoke haze.
Barges go gently down the Golden Horn,
the sky sheds all the seagulls over us.
The ship whistles and falls silent, blue on blue,
Karaköy Square, a child. Fish and bread!

Ell. 214   R.M.

ANGELS IN TOWN

It's autumn, the sky reddens early behind the mountains.
White-bearded elders with their silver rings
sit on a coffee-house bench facing the sunset,
silent, withdrawn in their deep loneliness.
An angel guards each shoulder, right and left.
One records sins, and grieves,
the other smiling notes their deeds of merit.
Girded with swords, in robes of taffeta,
they gently fan their wings in flight,
which folded, shape a curve of holy script.

It's autumn, the sky darkens early behind the mountains.

Ell. 215   R.C.

THE LIGHTS GO OUT

All the lights of the house go out.
The boy's eyes close.
Is there a passing moonbeam,
or is it the glimmer of fork and spoon,
the stove and chest, like a trembling star?
The pillow and cushion grow cold as a corpse.
They left the table a little before,
the door's open.
There's wine, but nobody drinking,
slices of bread, a chessboard,
the loser abandoned the game — the men like this,
the King surrounded, the Queen shivering in defeat.
Only the clocks keep ticking, rapid and steady,
big and little clocks
all night.

Ell. 221   R.C.

NOT SO

A skeleton ship, a church in ruins,
timeless remains,
something surviving from Byzantium
from the Middle Ages to our world.

Alien and calm, indifferent but aware,
distinct as a concrete thought,
at the point where the branch ends, the leaves —
and where the leaves end,
the cold and meaningless sky
with a thousand drooping sleepy eyes
kept watch.
Not so it seemed to us,
so distant, unconcerned, in such other worlds,
so like disdainful women lying languid,
skirts open to the groin.
There was an edge of bitterness on our tongue,
infinity's sour taste.
We, a mere luckless sultan who had lost his throne,
Prince Jem,
bereft of standards, janissaries, Istanbul,
languished in inconsolable grief.

Ell. 234   R.C.

NIKO'S COFFEEHOUSE

When he's not painting the rowboat Niko drinks raki.
Niko is quiet. The tables are spread with his silence.
These are his loneliness, these whitewashed walls, uneven and lumpy.
The ship he bought from a shop in Kostenje stands close by the samovar,
this picture is of the Piraeus, these lobsters from Batum,
these nets poured fish on the shore by the ton.
Niko in summers past, with seagulls screaming,
the swordfish and octopus loosed from the harpoon,
in the hottest of suns,
mixed mortar for his coffeehouse.
But the devilfish stay in the deep.
The grouper flattens his fins like a horse
in the hollowed sharp rock of Kefalos.
The purple barfish slowly play their fins and stare at Niko.
Grey clouds of mackerel move at the surface,
on the roof of the sea.
The glistening schooner's shadow strikes the seaweed, the
                                                    dark sponges.
Oh sea-bed, found at last, elusive bitch!
You're in that cloud of smoke, in tea,
on plate, in cupboard!
It's you Niko gives when he hands back the change,
he eats you, smokes you in his cigarette,
knows you and lies with you at nights.
A sail glides by the door. A crab
closes his eyes on a table in the corner.
A great red gurnet cuts the line and down he dives.
Like fish discarded and crushed, cast out from the nets to the sea,
Niko throws out memories with no beginning or end.
Dreams frolic underfoot like the coffeehouse kittens,
when you catch one you nurse it and stroke it.
Mother's away sunning herself on the bench.
Niko's far-off as well, still as the sea and its blue.

He sips his evening raki, the colour of clouds,
on the end of his fork a salty morsel of squid,
a crumb of dream on his plate, an olive,
he's deep in thought.
He roves with the blackeye and dances with the sea-bream.

Days when he lived with the stars come into his mind,
one-storeyed houses, roofs: a line of trawl-nets
goes down from north to south by moonlight,
heavy with Aegean winds.
The lighthouse beam divides us, and we shout:
'Make us a tea, Niko, and brew it strong!'
At every sip time multiplies, expands.
As you look, a terebinth tree at the window
becomes the harbours they entered long ago,
and an oleander, dwarfish and dusty, begins to smell sweet.
'Ah, Niko, if only the weather was always so fine!'
You're sitting and waiting. For whom do you wait?
The ones you're waiting for — why don't they come?
Those sounds you hear from over the sea —
is it the cities you long for,
those red and green glass globes in the greengrocer's shop,
the beaded curtains and coloured papers,
displays of melons, the little barber-shops?
Or do you miss the masts and decks and portholes?
Human beings are chancy as the weather.

Far off a cock crows, the sea glitters.
Havened in Niko's coffeehouse are men
facing away or sideways, playing cards.
When he's not painting the rowboat Niko drinks raki.
'Make us a tea, Niko, and brew it strong!' we shout,
'We've got the blues today!
— We've sorrows to drown.'

Ell. 224   R.C.

75

WIND AND WET

Those wet and windy nights
when I'm reduced to merely sound and echo
the sky's like a mill
which grinds down hope and joy, bright longing,
— whatever falls into its jaw.
Heavy and coarse,
a plough buries its blade in our hearts.
It furrows our fields, uproots
and tosses aside all likeness to grass and flower.
Our flesh is harrowed,
the seed of madness sinks deep.

Those wet and windy nights
when I'm reduced to merely sound and echo,
the sky's like a giant ship.
It empties the hold of its cargo,
and pours on the city
its burden, sticky and rotten.
Now remains no fence or wall or door.
Clouds like black leeches
with a thousand tongues and mouths
suck the last lingering light
from our fingertips, from our blood.

Ell. 235   R.C.

1509 EARTHQUAKE

It was a Time within a time,
whose wings were like an orange bird's.
When the earth shook, I was looking at Üsküdar
which tumbled from my window frame in blood and ruins.

They burned — my flower of chivalry — 300 horsemen:
in my vizier Mustafa's residence, baywindows, porches,
embroideries fell, gold leaves shed like scales,
stone clashed with stone, my Istanbul collapsed.

Giant figures were seen, Matthew, Luke,
John and the angels. On the ruined Byzantine walls
the double eagle, the new Testament

looked down disdainfully from the bluish skies.
Terrifying with their crosses, they looked down
at my quaking, helpless servants, afraid and alone.

Ell. 276   R.M. & R.C.

FATIH THE CONQUEROR'S PICTURE

A white cloud over the dome of Aya Sofia,
I watched it disappear. My honey-coloured prayer beads,
the amber days, leaves and hopes fell.
Knots of autumn rain streamed down the windows.

These shrouding kaftans were mine,
mine the horses' necks, the winds blew just right.
I stroked the stones of the city walls,
Istanbul was mine, its bastions were like me.

I ate off gold plates, I drank water
from a gold cup, I crossed the raging Danube.
I am Sultan Mehmet, Avni, with the proud crest of arms.

Captured in a picture I am a dwarf, but that's not me,
my scentless rose, my turban, my cold fur,
I'm wildly searching and searching everywhere.

Ell. 277   R.M.

A MAN

Before the last cloud in the sky had been completely swept away,
                                    before the plain was dark,
a red glow covered all around. The caique on the beach,
the dove on the branch was silent, we were silent.
The winding of the mantel clocks was done.
A woman withdrew her hand from the lentils on the tray,
                                    her eyes vacant.
No sound. The soup boiled. The earthenware jug sweats. The loaf
on the bread board asks to be sliced. As for the man
he's become invisible on the stone bench. Night breathes deeply
                                    into you,
go on, light up a cigarette, it's that wistful hour.

Çob. 153   R.M.

STARS

Nights we'd lie by the ditches and look at the stars.
Are those fireflies, or flies,
that flutter their transparent wings and buzz,
and stick all night on a reed,
where the crocuses are, and the water lilies spread on the stream?
This flashing light is their sparkle, this silence their noise.
But we, our heads on the grass, our eyes in the sky, the heavens,
dived in that milk-like water, the Milky Way.

Çob. 176   R.M.

ON THE LADDER

'Tomorrow the end of the world could come,' he said, 'the sea could climb the mountains, smash the wooden wharf and rowing boat, but since now the sea is still as a millpond, then feel the trawls strung together over us, and the sea dragging the hanging nets in the starry darkness.' He fell silent. A fish did a treble jump out of the water.
Then not a sound.

Çob. 183   R.M.

THE CAFÉ BY THE SEA
AT THE START OF THE SEASON

Spring steps into the plain, like a child learning to walk.
The sun is crisp. There's a milky fig taste in its rays.
The shacks open windows and doors to nature.
Tablecloths spread in the café. The washing
has to be secured with clothes-pegs or it will fly
off to the seagulls sleeping on the caiques by the jetty.
The café is completely deserted. A cat curled into a ball on the harbour wall.
A chair leans back on a cloud, in sleep.
One might come and ask for a strong tea,
a woman might crouch, putting her bundle on the ground, and
                                                wipe away her sweat,
a barefoot child, shoe-box on his shoulder might ask: 'Shoe shine, sir?'
All this will happen. Summer will come. The sky is raw, the blue fresh.
The chairs, the tables, the awning are on top of the sea.

Çob. 185   R.M.

80

CHILD AND DOG

Going through the grassy field left fallow:
if only there were a child, we'd walk Indian file,
he said, with a dog behind, and find a path through the reeds
to go down to the sea. But since there's no child or dog,
what use is it to go down to the sea?

Çob. 186   R.M.

SEASIDE

Carnations under the whitewashed wall, blue sky,
thistles and grass on the hillslope down to the sea,
a caique uncaulked for years.
From the wooden jetty let's look below
where the sunlight gleams in the water;
let's try skipping pebbles, three skips, four,
and whoever beats that
steals back to his childhood!
Past days beneath us upside down;
a hermit-crab shell,
the traveller gone, his haircloth abandoned,
empty and whorled
sinks into my palm.

Çob. 216   R.C.

81

THE WOMAN AND THE FISHING-BOAT

In the evening she gathered the children and went down
                                        to the house on the shore,
she crouched by the sea and 'Play,' she said, 'don't fight!'
If running and throwing stones is play,
the children played.
A cat looked on with big youthful eyes,
her kitten in a milky cloud,
the woman brooded deep in thought.
A fishing boat chugged up to the wooden quay.
A man landed, he took the woman by the hand,
he took the children and handed them on board.
He left a lapdog where the woman had crouched, he up and went.
We stayed on the shore alone with the dog.
Side by side we looked at the vanishing fishing boat,
                                        at its funnel and mast,
at the blue smoke billowing from the funnel.

Çob. 222   R.C.

OLD WIVES' TALE

Our village had winding ways, cypresses, cottages, courtyards,
slender minarets, towers, and arrow-shafts in the towers.
Our world had sevenfold cities under the earth,
you could leap on a black sheep's back down the blind well.
The umbrella tree was there, at the top the Phoenix nest,
the snake glided from tree to nest and every year ate the bird's young
before the prince stabbed it. There were sorcerers disguised as doves
who stripped and splashed in the spring, then in dove's feathers
returned to their cells. The forty thieves and giants
were not from our tales. A negro, enormous-lipped
sprang up beside you — I'll grant you whatever you wish.
Three-headed, seven-headed dragons died at one sword-thrust.
Youths fell in love and ran off with fairy women,
mothers pursued them, the sorceress changed the youths at once
                                                      to a garden,
and trick for trick, ruse against ruse, herself to a gardener.
The wicked were always defeated.
The Sultan's one grief, he was childless, had always a cure.
A wise man appeared by the fountain and offered an apple from his bosom,
if she ate it the Sultan's wife would give birth to a beautiful boy,
and the mare a fine foal.
The prince dreamt of a dancer, a laughing quince, and a pomegranate
                                                      that wept.
There was meat for the horse and hay for the lion, how about that!
We would have given hay to the horse and meat to the lion.
All obstacles overcome in the end, the poor boy becomes the
                                                      Sultan's vizier,
marries the princess, the wedding festivities last forty days and nights,
they live happily ever after and we go to our beds.
        Where has it all gone now?

Çob. 224   R.C.

83

MILKING TIME

'Put the peaches on the shelf, let the kitchen smell of peaches!'
the man said, and got off the bench and went to milk the cow.
The woman saw the cow looking at the pasture while it was being milked:
a galvanised bucket beneath; teats in his hands, side on
the man puffs as he brings down the milk cropped from clover and thyme,
black and white flecks in the clear evening.
She went to the kitchen, arranged the peaches on the shelf.
Now the flowerpot in the mirror, the embroidered pillow,
the light between the beams, the purple of the kilim,
now even the spiders smell of peaches,
the sky is peach-coloured, the clouds smell of peaches.

Çob. 230   R.M.

TONIGHT

Let them come no nearer,
but in the tremulous sunlight of autumn days
let them stay blue with the intervening mist,
sea, hill and roof.
But you,
my villagers, my daughters, my babies, come,
come near, a little nearer, nestle close.
In the coffeehouses, on the wooden benches,
let's sit close,
let's come to table, knee to knee on the rug,
let's eat our fill together from one dish.
Look! the wild geese pass with beating wings,
the poison-flower has scattered its blooms.
Close the shutters, light the stove,
tonight we've company.

Den. 85   R.C.

SEEING

Have you seen the transparency of a leaf,
Have you seen
    sunlight pass through the eye of a needle,
Have you seen
    the sea and the shore and all its days pass through the green,
Have you seen
    the leaf crossing the sea!

Look at the shadow of night on the wall.
Watch it pass through the wall,
life refracted like sunflame
through the grass.

Look at the leaves with your hands.
Feel with your eyes.
Grasp them and smell them.

Den. 107   R.C.

WORKERS CARRYING
BRICKS AND MORTAR

In black shorts, naked to the waist,
they were bearing the bricks and mortar of the building.
They were bearing the stars of the house on their shoulders,
the branches which would be seen from the window,
the neighbour's part,
the path lost in the trees.
They were bearing places of quiet and desire,
where we often hid to make love;
they were bearing corners, the stairhead,
the light from the kitchen to play on the hall,
a young girl suddenly dying
between two doors; perhaps summer's beginning,
perhaps flowerpots, fuchsia, Algerian violets,
they were bearing loneliness, kisses,
arguments, silences mingled with blackberries,
the joy of a craving for far-off places beyond the sea,
the bowed shoulders, the one in the armchair,
the one who'd walk in the hall,
the fragrant tree, the bubbling tea-kettle raised in the kitchen,
shedding its bark as it grows,
on the table the purslane and parsley, tomatoes,
the hand not reaching the spoon, the crumb caught in the throat,
the child to be born before he died
in an April rain with sun in his palm.
Don't let the tea grow cold, here's your favourite jam.
They were bearing that, look, just there
the place where hopes poured from our lives,
and slowly, slowly the house was rising
                    into its destiny.

But they — must be gone before sunset.

Den. 115   R.C.

87

FOR TODAY

Come my beauty,
close the door of today.
We did good work.
We kneaded bread with dreams,
with love,
we sprinkled roses on the cheese and olives.
Today was
glass doors, windows of cloud,
the ivory comb and embroidered headscarf.

Tomorrow the tree can shed its leaves
with scarcely a glance.

Dil. 13   R.C.

THE SEA, THE WOMAN AND THE OWL

The woman with the owl looks at us
with never a blink.
There's a coin on her open palm.
We and the fishermen look at her idly.
One of them flings a fish,
another pays no attention and mends his net.
Her eyes and hand stay open
and the eyes of the owl.
Suddenly the sea comes up
and pours its indigo blue
on owl and woman.

Without looking back
they return where they came from.
Blue deep blue.

Dil. 23   R.C.

TWO UNEMPLOYED

Let the moon's rising
be perfectly placed.
Don't show me the sea.

My hands in the handcuffs of exile,
the oleanders half-open,
don't show me the perfectly tilled earth.

These roads are long.
These roads go backwards.

Grief is a black snake.
Let the kebab-sellers be perfectly placed.

Don't sing love songs
of fire,
the smoke is blinding me.

Dil. 25   R.M.

OFF THE BACK OF A LORRY

Fallen off the back of a lorry,
water melons burst blood red,
black seeds scatter —
green heaps on the muddy road.
I see these dreams for you.
I fly to you from the earth.
I shed my leaves
while you turn your face from me.

You are poor, your nails stubby, hands
callussed, soles of feet cracked,
but your breasts are white from the fine flour
as you bake the flat bread in the clay oven
and put it on my table with the salt.
The fresh budding almond branches
of the purple evenings close over us.

Let's sleep below them.

Dil. 39   R.M.

HE DESCRIBES THE
COMING OF THE MUSE

She rises naked from her foamy table,
bringing green from the depths.
Pale with mud she comes,
like a guillotine south wind
dragging dead seabirds
to the wooden hut on the shore
where the divers drink coffee.

Rending her maidenhead she comes,
with the dizzying knockout speed of thought,
openhanded to beggars,
she comes with a half-articulate call.

Dil. 42   R.C.

91

ON SILENT SHORE

One day poems finish,
sea-urchins, octopi survive,
sweet basil behind glass.

One day hopes finish.
A horse cart in the shade,
the mare suckles its foal.

I saw all these things:
the mare, the coffee house, the vine.

You in your short skirt,
unaware of its significance,
were looking at me.
As for me, with unattainable speed,
I was scything the night that had begun into two.

I looked: the sea had finished,
the sand was bloody,
the doors creaking,
the roads, the narrow road, the pebbly roads
like the lifeless fingers of a dead hand.

I saw these things with my own eyes
on silent shore,
the blue seagulls' cries falling about me.

Dil. 46   R.M.

A HOPELESS CASE

I can't take you on my saddle.
I can't carry you off to the mountains —
I have no horse.

I have no double-barrelled shotgun.
My hands are by my side,
I can't shoot the green-crested duck.

I can't satisfy you.
I'm not spicy meatballs.
I'm in pain and suffering.

A purple kilim,
a blanket,
who or what
were my night fantasies!

Dil. 50   R.M.

OTHER HOMES

Barefoot, no slippers,
your nightshirt slipping over your knees,
I seemed to sense the smell of apricots.
A slice of Time the colour of apricots
divorced us from the other homes.

Dil. 51   R.M.

93

GHOST

When I'm dead I'll come.
I'll leap on a stone and come.
I'll shine in the candle of your room
behind the wet glass.
Through the heart of the shadows
I'll creep
and wait till all's quiet.
I'll not stay for the light of day,
I'll come with the rain.
Wait for me,
I'll be there.
When the hour strikes,
when the Other is gone,
when night descends,
I'll come.

Dil. 64   R.C.

INSCRIPTION

If you need to write again what you have written
translate it into another language and write,
because words are quicksilver
and do not settle easily.

We will never find again
one thousand stones, one thousand holes,
the flying carpet in the Thousand and One Nights
which flies only over Baghdad.

Here even the birds are taciturn.
They seem to miss their fruit.
They settle on the white wings of rowing boats
like angels on statues.

I brought you this rose,
I bought you this silver comb.
Carve an inscription on marble
with this stone-mason's chisel,
then roll it into the sea.

Dil. 72   R.M.

THE POPLAR

When they were felling the poplar
it stood for the last time
upright and tall in air
in all its leaves,
then toppled —
leaves for a long time shivered,
branches twitched,
hens scattered wide.

Claytiles don't hold with poplars,
only mud-roofs
drink from the welling sap.

Dil. 75   R.C.

TREE ANECDOTE

That year the cherry blossoms of the spring
instead of staying to fruit
were dropping off untimely.
The garden was deserted,
I was not there, nor you,
and these lines perhaps had not yet been written.

A horseman came from the South.
He looked at the blossoms on the ground.
He hung his whip on the tree.
He turned his horse's head and went.

Dil. 89   R.C.

96

DISPERSED

My memories live in a mountain village
of grassy slopes,
my dreams in a sea-town,
my hopes in the saltless sea
of Istanbul.
I pull it over me like a quilt.
The Maiden's Tower, a mermaid
sunning on the bank,
a woman combs her hair
bending her head like the sun's ears of grain.
When I reap them I'll bind a sheaf
and bring it to Üsküdar
among a thousand years of people,
young, old and middle-aged.
In the rain beginning
on a May afternoon
I'll open the lock of all glass.

Every reflex answering light with light
is close to me.
Look, a ferryboat draws near
to my beam.

Dil. 96   R.C.

ON SEA-URCHIN ROCK

The fish that are my friends
I harpooned and threaded on the wire,
and sold them
at the fish-seller's counter.

That day in the open on sea-urchin rock,
my knees all bloody,
a little bream on my harpoon:
I skinned it and bit into it
with glee.

I bit into the flesh of my people on sea-urchin rock,
I bit into the sun, the salt, nature;
all the folk songs of the Anatolian poets,
especially my Yunus Emre and my Pir Sultan Abdal.

Like painting in a paint book
I mixed blue for the sea,
sunk into indigo,
I was a crab, an octopus.
I opened the door of the 40th room
with that missing little skeleton-key.
I felt the essence of my existence
on sea-urchin rock in the sun.

Dil. 132   R.M.

98

OUTSIDE

I went into the telephone box.
When I came out, hey life!
Tree, road, oleander;
the summer day perfectly poised,
and I realised that the sea and sand
were waiting for me by the coffee house.

Koca 13   R.M.

WALL

On the whitewashed wall
I wrote your name in charcoal,
then I drew a ship on top
and fish row on row.
The ship picked you up and took you off,
I spat at the blue.
I rubbed out the seas angrily.

Koca 14   R.M.

TO LET

There were fairy houses in the old days
which no one would rent.
Noise all night,
merriment through till morning,
a candle flame roving at the windows.

Fearfully we passed them,
those white tumble-down lodges
among the pine trees.
They were more like death,
and we'd ring the bell, then run

on the pebbled road lined by cherry trees:
childhood with the heart thumping.

But now — no mystery, no secret!

Koca 20   R.M.

FERRY

The Bosphorus ferry smoke
rakes the caiques.

A seagull by the quay
soars and swoops
after a discarded mackerel.

Where's this ferry going?
Tell me, friends.

Mustn't get the wrong one: this one's for the Bosphorus.

The Beshiktash ferry has a carved cradle.
The Beshiktash ferry is different.

Koca 28   R.M.

HIGH STYLE

Leave the stove to me, I'll light it.
I'll fetch the wood.
You drink your tea.
Enjoy your morning,
let the sleep glide from your eyes,
like the smoke rising from the mountain peak.
Tuck your legs under.
Tuck in the cloud within you,
take it easy.
Be like the cities drunk on the scorching sun
and the rippleless blue sea.
Gently fondle your breasts.
Cast a glance at the newspaper on the sofa.
This style of living suits my minx.

Koca 31   R.M.

PADISHAH

Selim the First loved blood
Selim the Second — wine
Selim the Third — music and poetry
Selim the Fourth never existed —
Thank God!

Koca 38   R.M.

LIMETREES

I have begun to forget those places.
The road to the sea is waning,
the house on top of the hill,
the umbrella tree above the yogurt-seller's,
the fishmonger's slab in the market.
First they fade, then they're wiped out.

As though I was looking
from a vehicle speeding away,
first the image grows distant, then vanishes.

The pictures of our past are on the wing.

One thing only never grows less nor ends,
but gradually stronger —
the swooning smell of limetrees in May.

Koca 42   R.C.

INSCRIPTIONS ON A RUINED FOUNTAIN

Inscriptions on a ruined fountain,
left over in the mosque courtyard
look at me from afar.

These are remnants from the fine fingers of the Master,
from the Poet, from the favourite Odalisque,
hair sweet-smelling, lips for kissing.

Time, the enemy of art and life,
withered them like autumn branches
which had shed their yellow fallen leaves.

Koca 56   R.M.

WAITING

The woman looks out of the window,
the man returns home,
the child plays in the street,
the clock ticks on the wall.
Evening is waiting at the door,
a yellow evening, a good evening.

Koca 60   R.M.

PRESSURE

The woman is poised on the brink of loneliness,
the man looks depressed.
A blind light burns in the room,
five huge storeys stacked above
on top of that roof, on top of that sky.
The black-faced ceiling weighs down,
the walls close in, close in.
They look up
trying to estimate the load they carry.

Koca 62   R.M.

A GLANCE AT THE SUMMER EVENING

Outside the sun is setting.
Evening's flood overwhelms the city.
This most stagnant hour of the day
proceeds dragging its skirts.
Cheat, thief, vagabond, pimp
roll up their sleeves, the bar's full.
The whore's waiting for a client.
As for you, your windows are open,
from the hot smells of summer
and from a distance you look at a time far off.
The blue of the weather
shudders in the room's loneliness.

Koca 63   R.M.

1619

A comet appeared that year:
a bloody light cluster in the sky,
curved as a scimitar,
from east to west
A huge-headed snake
hung over Istanbul.

Istanbul was afraid.

Koca 67   R.M.

THE LODOS MAN

Walking the streets skilled but out of work,
our daily bread depends on the whim of lodos, the south wind.
If the wind blows benignly I don't go hungry.
All day long I'm out of my mind.

But when evening comes the sun sets,
my loneliness sharpens a little.
The night seas never end,
it's hard to make it through the night.

The sun's wine enters my bloodstream.
I slice bread for the hungry.
I set off on long journeys.

I walk and sink in and out of dreams.
I enter the bridal chamber with the sea-maidens.
I pick up golden coins on the beach.

Koca 69   R.M.

AFTER YOU

After you had moved away
the taste went out of life.
The coffee house in the old wooden home is empty,
the familiar fountain is sharp as a needle,
my footsteps retreat.
The passengers come off the ferry, you're not there.
The crowds come out of the cinema, you're not there.
Perhaps the roll-seller won't come round in the evening.
Old sounds we used to know together make me restless:
I keep looking for you at the window
as though you're going to open it,
you seem to be leaning out
over and over again.

Koca 72   R.M.

THE FOX

Outlined by branches and leaves the fox
glides from his tree,
like a blue smoke when it's evening.
Dogs follow behind him.
They run and run on the plain
to the other end of loneliness.

Koca 89   R.C.

GARBAGE

The shadows of women who pick the garbage
for just a dead crow,
fall before me in the darkening street.
I seize them and throw them on the garbage.

I throw the passing day to the garbage,
everything lived and used,
the seabird's wing, the penknife's blade,
green plums on the plate
are going to the garbage, my dear, to the garbage.

The starved horse and his cart are going,
our hair and nails and loves,
the fish-heads we ate,
the chicken bones, lemon peel,
sardine tins, the newspaper we read —
we're going to the garbage, every day a bit more,
to the place of the rubbish-heaps.

I look: a broken bottle
suddenly catching the blue of the sky,
winks on and off like a lighthouse.

It's going to the garbage.

Koca 94   R.C.

TRUTHS

I cannot say that the sea's blue
is bluer than the sky's,
and that the trees are red.
Ship ahoy!
A ship on the roof.
A ship on the wall.

I cannot say
that caiques are like insects,
and smell of roses or jasmine.

I cannot say, I cannot say
I carried a soul,
that my days in the garden
are warmed by the sun,
and that leaves fall in early summer.

I listen to the birds of a distant season.
I glow in my mind.
I enter a city
seen only in dreams,
with you on the back of my horse.

I cannot say
that I know tomorrow will come.

Koca 98   R.M.

LAMENT FOR A DAY NOT GONE

A pure day, or the white remnant
of a summer night. The wisteria, the trellis,
the line stretching from
the hedge to the acacia,
paused with the sun in the palm.
A line of water on the pupils of my eyes.

I looked at my reflection:
a tang of salt mixed with grasses.
I looked from inside the acacia
from inside my love, together with the sky
purified from stone and earth.
If it goes it will never come back.

The whole family was snagged on a fishing line,
flies buzzing,
The down-and-out fisherman
passed through the silence of the reed-fringed waters.
A window with two shutters open like wings,
sky in his basket.

The sky smelled of seaweed,
a summer covered in vine leaves
in the day's dreams with the whole family.
We were a sea foaming into the evening,
tired birds on our shoulders.
For days we were that day.

Koca 99   R.M.

BAY

Look at the play of the caique on the water.
Come to the green and red.
There are both sea and sky on the balcony,
find the houses' shadow.

Reeds and seaweed sway on the bottom,
snails and sea-urchins,
crabs eye to eye,
fish face to face,
bivalve molluscs,
sea insects and fleas.

The flag fluttering above,
seagull lost in smoke,
the ferry's steam whistle,
a shudder through the tips of branches,
a stirring in the waters.

Koca 100   R.M.

HAIR

A man hands the money to the barber
self-consciously looking at
his left-overs, the hair and cotton wool
on the chair and floor.

The next client waiting his turn
takes his place in the chair.

The boy sweeps up the hair,
folds the towels.
A narcissus-coloured time —
the canary sings in the cage,
sunny days in the mirrors.

The man goes out of the shop,
a whistle on his lips,
and something missing inside.

Koca 101   R.M.

GARDEN AND SEA

A boat passes through the plum trees
trailing a cloud.
The smoke's left behind,
a seagull flies above,
a man holds the tiller.

We're going back in time:
in the small garden of a summer house
the milkman makes his way over the stones.
The horse waits at the door,
a blue evil-eye bead round its neck —
flowers flowers flowers.

Our table is laid:
tomatoes, raki, bran-bread,
watercress and sea.

Koca 102   R.M.

MY GRANDMOTHER

You could see the sea from my grandmother's
tiny white house.
The tinkling would ring
when people came and went.
Ortaköy Mosque was opposite.
Grandma with her cat on her lap
used to look out of the window.
Her face was fine and pale as parchment.
Her cardigan smelled of lilac,
her garden of jasmine.

Koca 111   R.M.

LETTER

The swing flies to the sky,
the kite glides,
the balloon takes off,
the children are playing on the sand.

A woman squats down in a meadow,
two naughty boys beside her.
She's writing a letter from her heart
which is pierced by a deadly splinter:
'It's outrageous, everything's gone up in smoke.
Save me, I'm swamped'.

The calves are well fed,
the crows are tame.
Time sparkles over the grass
like the sea in summer.

Koca 112   R.M.

114

LOOKING

When I lift the lid of the pot
and look in,
it's not that I'm hungry,
and not at all that I'm curious,
but because to look at food
is a passion as old,
I'd say,
as looking at the dead.
What do you think?

Koca 113   R.C.

A WIND

It seemed we were in our house in Istanbul.
It is summer. We are in the garden,
a cat wandering underfoot
poking his nose in the food. We chase him,
he leaps through the grass and away.
I pick up a musical instrument,
but I don't know how to play it.
I can't play.
Suddenly I see you by my side.
You haven't died.
We are all alive,
friends and neighbours in good shape.
A wind blows from the mountain,
the purple mountain behind us.
All the trees rock.

Koca 117   R.C.

THE FISHERMAN AND THE SEA

Yesterday the sea was silent,
today it's muttering,
tomorrow it could be raving and foaming,
but the fisherman who lives on his own
occasionally looks into space
and never talks for days on end.

Koca 121   R.M.

RUKIYE

Rukiye, you've got golden eyes.
Your hair, Rukiye,
blows like the sunny sea winds.

Wearing a cotton print dress,
wooden shoes on your feet,
you're washing the courtyard floor
with soap and water on a summer day.
Your breasts are showing:
I can't stand it!

Away from you life's not worth living —
I'm a broken empty man away from you,
in love with the sea and Rukiye.
Without Rukiye, without the sea,
everything goes to rack and ruin,
and I don't sleep well.

Koca 122   R.M.

116

Feyyaz Kayacan Fergar

Feyyaz Kayacan Fergar, who died in April 1993, was a close friend of Oktay Rifat from their days together as students in Paris, and took a personal interest in the publication of this English collection. He himself had published his translations of Oktay Rifat in his anthology *Modern Turkish Poetry* (Rockingham Press, 1992) and in *Contemporary Turkish Literature,* edited by Talat S. Halman (Farleigh Dickinson University Press, 1982).

We feel it fitting that these fine translations should be included in this book.

POEM

In the evening breeze in the parish
time is like a birdcage: slowly
and gently it sways in the window
over the back garden of the red-painted house,
the house smelling of tobacco, of bread.
And the birds sing: chipet, chipet, chitalinya.
The sun goes down, we withdraw to our rooms,
the trees, our house, the world, together we gravitate.

F.K.F

FLAME

In the morning of adventures outgrown
chestnut trees resume my childhood.
The candle-flame touches
birds bygone and quivers.

F.K.F

THE STONES

All night long in my tightly folded hands
I must have kept my shivering stones.
Waking in the morning I saw them standing:
the pigeon on the eaves, the cat on the threshold,
the cloud on the roofs.
My loneliness was ashore in the mirror.
Waking in the morning I saw it standing
over sun and tree.

F.K.F

FLOWER SHOP

I fed them with the milk of trees,
I made them grow this high.
They are my orphans, my near ones,
they wave hands from afar, fret about.
In voiceless smells
their world dwindles.

F.K.F.

GIRLS

Girls are green and sometimes blue,
they point toward the sky the streets
of our towns. Girls are our sailing clouds
we look at, crouched at the bottom of walls.
Without thinking we think of a port, we make
our way through trees, there comes the sound of the sea,
a pomegranate shows us her breasts.
Through the door half-open
we see in the house
the staircase helping up a lovely carpet.

Girls are green and sometimes blue.

                              F.K.F   *Ell. 220*

EARTH

I stepped on the wet earth.   Suddenly
        I was a tree, I was bud, I was knot.
            Toward the sun I turned
my leaf-drawn face.   I heard that breeze
        in the headlong sky.   Come close,
lovely girls, come close and with linked hands
        dance in circles around me.

                    F.K.F

IN MY SLEEP

I found it in my sleep.   It was
standing in the green of the grass.
Scant and sad, like the face of a child,
small endlessly,
it was looking at a bygone part of me;
a swallow softly brushing it
flew over, singing.
Oh I loved it so, tears singing in my eyes.

Then, like the others, it disappeared.

F.K.F